Little Sheldon Celebrates Fall

Written by Lisa Trout   Illustrated by Jordan Raymond

A special thanks to Brielle and Chad.

Your enthusiastic responses to our work
were very appreciated.

The wind blew in this morning, through my open window,
A leaf floats in and lands on my pillow.
I sprung from my bed to see what was the matter,
"It must be Fall," I said as I watched the leaves swirl
and gather.

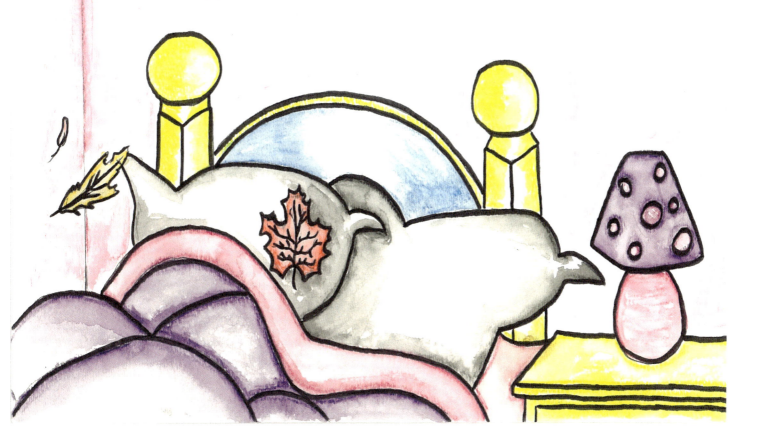

I helped Mommy pick me a dress with pink and brown.
We ate a healthy breakfast before heading into town.
Mommy made us baskets all sparkly and shiny.

Hers was really big
and mine
was really tiny.

The apple orchard smells so sweet,
Once a tiny seed, is now a yummy treat.
Our baskets piled high and low,
One game of apple peek-a-boo before we go.

Looking for a pumpkin shape with a special glow,
Off to the pumpkin patch we go.
Digging out the seeds and making pumpkin pie,
Excited for new recipes for me to try.

On our way
back to our house,
Playing in the leaves
was the cutest
little mouse.

We fill our arms with
a hundred leaves in all,
This is my favorite
part of Fall.

What can we do
with a hundred leaves
in a pile?
Maybe a votive
is worthwhile!

Let's put the leftover leaves in a compost to rest
Because nourishing the soil is what leaves
do best.

Now we are ready to start.
Using healthy ingredients is always smart.

Apples, cinnamon and banana in a bowl,
Having a lot of choices is a great goal.

Next, we make a
light mousse
pumpkin pie,
Using orange from
real pumpkin
instead of food dye.

Pecans, pumpkins and coconut cream,
Mommy and I make a great team.

A day of planning is all done,
Dinner with family will be so fun.
We get to share all the things we have made,
And tell stories of all the games we have played.

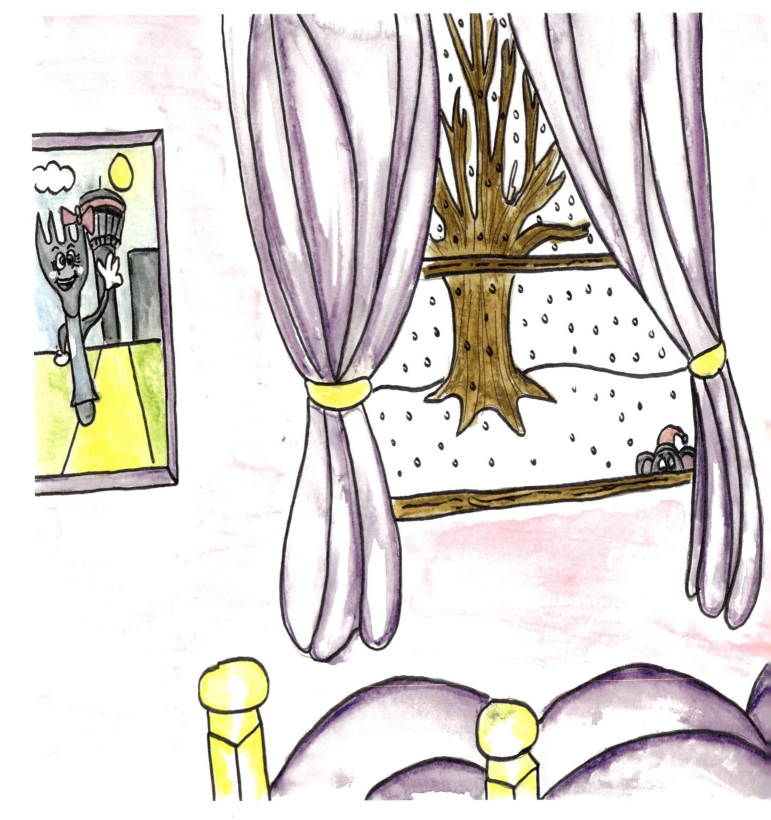

From leaves to pumpkins to apples galore,
What will be our next recipe to explore?
As the seasons are changing and snow lightly falls,
I can't wait to try recipes that will surely warm us all!

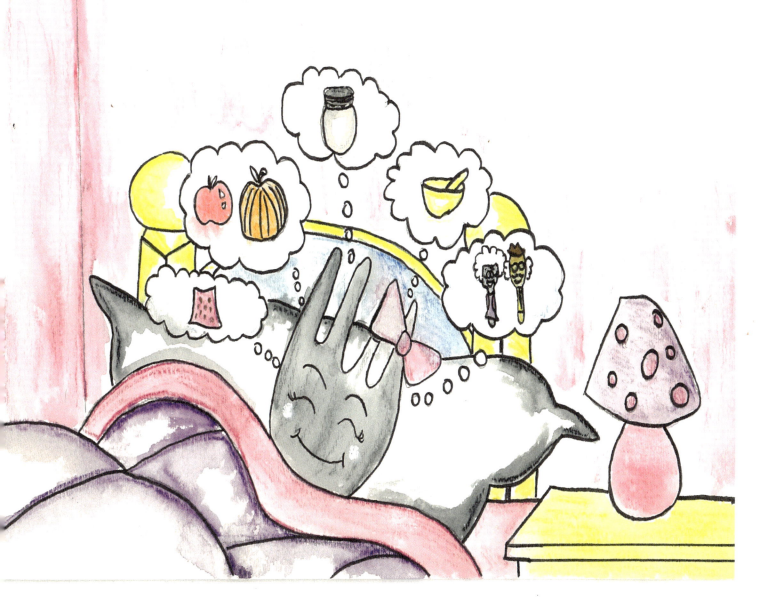

Light Mousse Pumpkin Pie

Pumpkin Filling:
1 cup pure pumpkin
1 cup coconut milk
1 teaspoon of pumpkin pie spice
1 teaspoon vanilla
3 tablespoons of maple syrup (more or less if desired)
Pinch of salt

Coconut cream:
1 can coconut milk
1 teaspoon of vanilla
3 tablespoons of maple syrup (more or less if desired)

Candied Pecans:
Handful of pecans
1 teaspoon of coconut oil
1 tablespoon of maple syrup
Pinch of salt

Step 1: Make the Filling

Add coconut milk and pumpkin to a sauce pan on medium heat, stirring constantly so that it does not burn. Stir in a pinch of salt, vanilla and maple syrup. Cook until it reaches a slight boil, reduce heat, stirring constantly until it thickens. Remove from heat, place in a bowl, let cool a couple minutes, then cover with plastic wrap. Place in fridge for a few hours to cool and firm.

Step 2: Make the Coconut Cream

Chill coconut milk for at least an hour. Open can and remove only solid part of milk, leaving as much juice as possible in the can. Beat the milk with the vanilla and maple syrup until smooth.

Step 3: Make the Candied Pecans

Melt a bit of coconut oil in a medium sauce pan. Drop a handful of pecans, 1 tablespoon of maple syrup and a pinch of salt. Roast, stirring constantly until lightly toasted. Place on a plate and set aside to cool.

Step 4: Assemble

Once all steps are completed, you can begin to layer your light mousse pumpkin pie. Layer with pumpkin filling, coconut cream and pecans. You can add a healthy graham crumb layer if you choose.

Visit www.LittleChewz.ca for more healthy recipes

Apple Pie Smoothie

Ingredients:

1/2 of a banana
2 pitted dates
1 cup of almond milk
1 sliced apple with peel
1 teaspoon of pumpkin spice
2 tablespoons of pecans
Handful of ice (optional)

Directions:

Mix all ingredients in a blender and serve.
You can add other ingredients for added nutrition such as a spoonful of
hemp seeds for protein or flax seed oil for omega fats.

Craft Idea: Mason Jar Votive

Supply List:

1-2 mason jars
Fresh leaves that have been collected from outside
Paintbrush
Ribbon or twine
Glue sealer
Non-flammable electronic candle

Directions:

Place leaves on outside of mason jar and paint with glue sealer.
Wrap the top of the jar with ribbon or twine and let dry. Place
a non-flammable electronic candle inside and place outside!

5 Healthy Tips To Eat And Live More Locally And Sustainably In The Fall

1- Apples are in season until November! Take full advantage of eating the peel of organic apples as the peel contains pectin and flavonoids and is rich in fiber and antioxidants. Take a visit to the apple orchard and try our apple pie smoothie! This one calls for the peel.

2 - Enjoy pumpkins from October to February! They are rich in potassium fiber and vitamin B! Try our light mousse pumpkin pie, in which you have the option of using real pumpkin from the pumpkin patch!

3 - Try sweet potato pumpkins! Sweet potatoes are in season from September to December and are high in vitamin A and iron. Cut the potato into medallions, stamp with a pumpkin cookie cutter, bake and eat as is, or top with a bit of cinnamon.

4 - Replace your sugar with dates! Dates are in season from September to December, are high in fiber and are a great source of potassium. We used dates to replace some of the sugar in the recipes of this book. Dates are a great addition to fall foods as they go well with cinnamon, vanilla, nuts and pumpkin.

5 - Don't forget to grab a blanket to warm up instead of turning up the heat in your house! This will not only save energy but it is more sustainable and creates a happier planet!

Made in the USA
San Bernardino, CA
07 November 2019